Chop and Chip

Written by Caroline Green

Collins

thing to cut with

buzz and chop

thing to cut with

buzz and chop

push it

thick log chunks

push it

thick log chunks

a man

. . . .

chips fill the van

a man

chips fill the van

/ch/

/ng/

 Review: After reading

Use your assessment from hearing the children read to choose any GPCs, words or tricky words that need additional practice.

Read 1: Decoding

- Use grapheme cards to make any words you need to practise. Model reading those words, using teacher-led blending.
- Look at the "I spy sounds" pages (14–15) together. Ask the children to point out as many things as they can in the picture that begin or end with the /ch/ sound. (*chipper, chips (wood), chips (food), cherries, chocolate, cheese, chess, peach, branch*) Next, ask the children to point out as many things as they can in the picture that end with the /ng/ sound. (*hanging (bat), wings, fangs, singing (bird), ring, ping pong*)
- Ask the children to follow as you read the whole book, demonstrating fluency and prosody.

Read 2: Vocabulary

- Look back through the book and discuss the pictures. Encourage the children to talk about details that stand out for them. Use a dialogic talk model to expand on their ideas and recast them in full sentences as naturally as possible.
- Work together to expand vocabulary by naming objects in the pictures that children do not know.
- Read pages 7 and 11. Discuss the difference between **chunks** and **chips**. Discuss what the machine on pages 10 and 11 is doing, and how it breaks up big bits into little bits.

Read 3: Comprehension

- Ask the children whether they have seen someone chopping a tree. Encourage them to describe what happened. Discuss how people called tree surgeons help us. They cut trees to keep the surrounding area safe, and to keep trees healthy. Alternatively, discuss any trees they have seen and the size of their trunks and branches.
- Reread pages 2 and 3. Ask: What noise is the machine making? (***buzz***) Talk about other machine noises the children have heard. Are they the same or different?